JOHN
GLENN

JOHN GLENN
SPACE PIONEER

CARMEN BREDESON

A Gateway Biography
The Millbrook Press
Brookfield, Connecticut

Cover photographs courtesy of Reuters/Pierre DuCharme/Archive Photos and NASA

Photographs courtesy of © AFP/Corbis: p. 6; Archive Photos: pp. 9 (CNP), 20, 32, 35 (Reuters/Win McNamee), 40 (Reuters/Mike Segar); AP/Wide World Photos: pp. 3, 12, 15, 17, 26, 33; © 1978 General Motors Corporation: p. 13; Corbis/Bettmann-UPI: pp. 19, 22, 24, 31; NASA: pp. 37, 39, 42.

Library of Congress Cataloging-in-Publication Data
Bredeson, Carmen.
John Glenn : space pioneer / Carmen Bredeson.
p. cm. — (A Gateway biography)
Includes bibliographical references and index.
Summary: A biography of former Senator John Glenn, who orbited the earth in 1962 and became the oldest man to go into space in 1998.
ISBN 0-7613-1719-8 (lib. bdg.)
1. Glenn, John, 1921- —Juvenile literature. 2. Astronauts—United States—Biography—Juvenile literature. 3. Legislators—United States—Biography—Juvenile literature. [1. Glenn, John, 1921- . 2. Astronauts. 3. Legislators.] I. Title. II. Series.
TL789.85.G6 B74 2000
629.45'0092—dc21 [B] 99-059775

Published by The Millbrook Press, Inc.
2 Old New Milford Road
Brookfield, Connecticut 06804
www.millbrookpress.com

JOHN
GLENN

Seventy-seven-year-old John Glenn as he makes his way to the space shuttle *Discovery* on October 29, 1998. It had been more than thirty-six years since he had been the first American in space, and now he would be the oldest person to travel there.

OCTOBER 29, 1998—FINALLY THE BIG DAY HAD ARRIVED! Liftoff of the space shuttle *Discovery* was just hours away. In the crew quarters at Kennedy Space Center in Cape Canaveral, Florida, seven excited astronauts were gathered around the breakfast table. They were talking about their upcoming mission, which was called STS-95. This mission had been getting a lot of media attention because one of the crew members, 77-year-old John Glenn, would be the oldest person ever to fly in space.

Thirty-six years earlier, on February 20, 1962, Glenn had accomplished another first. He was the first American astronaut to orbit Earth. His flight aboard *Friendship 7* made history as the United States blasted into the space age.

Several reporters asked John Glenn if he was more nervous in 1962 or 1998. He told them, "I think I was probably more nervous back in those days because we did not know much about spaceflight. . . . We were sort of feeling our way and

★ JOHN GLENN'S SPACE MISSIONS ★

	FRIENDSHIP 7	DISCOVERY
Date flown	Feb. 20, 1962	Oct. 29–Nov. 7, 1998
Altitude	162 miles (261 km)	325 miles (523 km)
Orbits	3	144
Length of flight	4 hrs., 55 min.	213 hrs., 45 min.
Distance flown	75,679 miles (121,843 km)	3,600,000 miles (5,796,000 km)
Crew space	36 cubic feet (1.02 cubic meters)	2,325 cubic feet (65.8 cubic meters)
Spacecraft length	6 feet 10 inches (2.1 meters)	122 feet (37.2 meters)
Windows	1	10
Glenn's age	40	77

finding out what would happen to the human body in space...."

Before Glenn and the *Discovery* crew could get off the ground, they had to suit up. First, each astronaut put on a *diaper*! Diapers were necessary because once the launch/entry suits were on, they could not be removed until the shuttle reached orbit. Sometimes launches were delayed for several

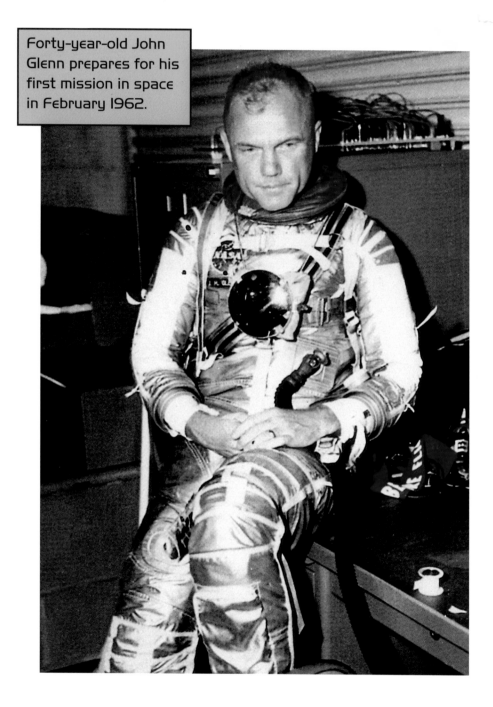

Forty-year-old John Glenn prepares for his first mission in space in February 1962.

hours and a full bladder during liftoff was very uncomfortable. Long underwear went on over the diaper, followed by socks. Then came the bright orange suits, which weigh 90 pounds (41 kilograms). Inflatable sections in the pants press on the legs and abdomen to protect the astronauts from pressure changes during liftoff and reentry.

Once dressed, the seven bulky astronauts filed out of the crew quarters and boarded a bus that took them to the launch site. *Discovery* was waiting for them at pad 39-B. STS-95 mission commander Curtis Brown, pilot Steve Lindsey, Dr. Scott Parazynski, and Pedro Duque pulled themselves across a ladder and climbed into their seats in the cockpit. Stephen Robinson, Dr. Chiaki Mukai, who in 1994 had become the first Japanese woman in space, and John Glenn struggled into their seats in the crew cabin.

Handholds and footrests are built into the shuttle to make the climb easier. Still, getting into the seats, which are reclining on their backs, is a challenge. Imagine that one of your kitchen chairs is lying on its back several feet off of the ground and you have to climb into it wearing a 90-pound suit!

When the final countdown began, spectators in the NASA viewing area heard the loudspeakers boom out: "Ten, nine, eight, seven, six, five, four, three, two, one, and liftoff of *Discovery* with a crew of six astronaut heroes and one American legend." Among those watching the liftoff were John Glenn's wife of 55 years, Annie, their daughter Lyn, son David, and teenage grandsons, Zachary and Daniel. Thousands more watched from the roads and beaches surrounding Kennedy Space Center. As *Discovery* soared through the sky, NBC's Tom Brokaw said on the air, "I don't know what *your* grandfather is doing today, but John Glenn is on his way to space."

Eight and a half minutes after liftoff, *Discovery* entered Earth's orbit going 17,500 miles (28,175 kilometers) per hour. Inside the crew cabin the pressures of acceleration were gone and everything was weightless. Curt Brown watched as John Glenn unfastened his straps and began to float. He reported to Mission Control, "Let the record show John has a smile on his face, and it goes from one ear to the other." John Glenn was finally back in space after 36 years!

Glenn's interest in flying and space didn't begin with the space race in the 1960s. It went way back to his childhood in Ohio during the 1920s.

WHEN JOHN HERSCHEL GLENN JR. WAS BORN IN CAMBRIDGE, Ohio, on July 18, 1921, the world was a very different place than it is today. The Wright brothers had made the first successful airplane flight just 18 years before. Charles Lindbergh's solo flight across the Atlantic would not happen until 1927. During the 1920s, passenger air travel was beginning to be popular in the United States, but it was often slow and unreliable.

Among John Glenn's favorite boyhood toys were small metal airplanes, which he held out of the car window on family outings to make the propellers spin. As he got older, he built

When this picture was taken of John Glenn in 1925, people were just beginning to see the possibilities of flight. Charles Lindbergh's historical first solo flight across the Atlantic Ocean was still two years away. Who would have dreamed that this four-year-old would one day be the first American in space?

airplane models out of paper and balsa wood. When the family visited nearby Columbus, Ohio, John often asked his dad to stop by the airport so he could watch the planes take off and land. When he was about nine years old, John and his dad took a ride in the back of a small plane. Glenn later said, "We went up and circled around Cambridge, Ohio. I was fascinated with flying from then on."

During his teens, John Glenn was also fascinated with cars. Luckily his father owned a Chevrolet dealership in New Concord, Ohio, where the family had moved in 1923. Out on the car lot was a maroon 1929 Chevrolet convertible that had been there for months. When John was 16, his father gave the

When it was new, John Glenn's car, "The Cruiser," a 1929 Chevrolet convertible, looked like this.

beat-up old car to him. Glenn remembers that the car "wasn't worth more than about 50 bucks, and in fact it wouldn't run when he gave it to me. And the top was long since rotted away. When it rained . . . the water would collect on the floor. So I bored a hole in the floor and let the water run out."

The car, which was named "The Cruiser," wouldn't go very fast either. According to Glenn, "The thing would only run about 40 miles (64 kilometers) an hour wide open, so you couldn't get in too much trouble with it." In spite of its drawbacks, The Cruiser was very popular because not many teenagers had cars in 1937. John's friends piled into the convertible on weekends to go to the movies or to school dances. One of the people who spent a lot of time riding around in the old Chevy was Anna "Annie" Castor.

John was just three years old and Annie was four when they first met. Their parents were friends and got together often for family dinners and celebrations. As they got older, John and Annie spent most of their free time together. John Glenn later said, "There's never been a time in our lives when we didn't know each other. Everything we've been through, we've been through together."

Annie Castor and John Glenn attended New Concord High School. He played trumpet in the band and lettered in football, basketball, and tennis. He was also president of the junior class and sang in the choir. No wonder the yearbook caption under John's picture called him the "busiest" and "all-around popular boy." Glenn made pretty good grades, but they were not exceptional. His mother, who was a former teacher,

Annie Castor and John Glenn were childhood friends, high school sweethearts, and got married while they were in college.

thought her son might make better grades if he spent less time on sports and social activities.

In 1939, John Glenn and Annie Castor graduated from New Concord High School and enrolled in Muskingum College, a small Presbyterian school in New Concord. John began working on a degree in chemical engineering while Annie studied music. During their freshman year in college, the Civil Aeronautics Authority began a Pilot Training Program at some schools in the United States, including Muskingum College. Students could learn how to fly as part of their college work and earn physics credits at the same time.

War had broken out in Europe in 1939, and the United States wanted to make sure extra pilots were trained to fly in case America got involved in the war. Since John Glenn was already interested in airplanes, he enrolled in the program. "I was sold on flying as soon as I had a taste of it," according to Glenn, who earned his pilot's license after completing the Muskingum course.

During Glenn's junior year in college, a Japanese force of more than 300 planes attacked Pearl Harbor, Hawaii, killing or wounding thousands of United States soldiers. The day after the December 7, 1941, attack, war was declared on Japan by President Franklin Roosevelt and the United States Congress.

John Glenn left college, joined the United States Navy, and started learning how to be a combat pilot. After earning his wings in Corpus Christi, Texas, on March 31, 1943, he switched from the Navy to the Marine Corps. Before Glenn was sent overseas, he returned to Ohio to marry Annie on April

In 1941, when this picture was taken, John was twenty-one years old and had just earned his pilot's license. At the end of that year, the United States would enter World War II and John would leave college to become a Navy pilot.

6, 1943. During the next year, John Glenn flew 59 missions over the Japanese-occupied Marshall Islands in the Pacific Ocean. He was awarded ten Air Medals and two Distinguished Flying Crosses for his service in the war.

When World War II ended in 1945, Glenn remained in the Marines, where he served as a test pilot and flight instructor for the next five years. Then, in 1950, the United States once again got involved in a war, this time in Korea. John Glenn requested combat duty and flew 90 missions in Korea. During one of the missions, his F9F Panther jet was hit and a dinner-plate-size hole was punched in the tail. The plane went into a dive, and Glenn had to use all of his skill as a pilot to avoid a crash. After flying his crippled plane back to base and landing safely, he said, "It was the closest I ever came to crashing in my life." For his bravery during combat in the Korean War, John Glenn earned two more Distinguished Flying Crosses and another eight Air Medals.

While her husband was serving in the Marine Corps, Annie Glenn stayed busy raising the couple's two children. David was born on December 13, 1945, followed by Lyn, who was born on March 19, 1947.

With the end of the Korean War in 1953, John Glenn's combat duty was finished. His flying days were far from over, though. Glenn attended test pilot school and graduated in August 1954. For the next five years he spent his days flying experimental aircraft higher and faster than they had ever been flown before.

John Glenn poses with Annie, their daughter Lyn, and son David at the completion of his 1957 flight from California to New York, in which he broke the cross-country speed record.

Soviet citizens view *Sputnik I* at an exhibition in Moscow in 1958, a year after its historic orbit.

On July 16, 1957, Glenn broke the cross-country speed record when he flew a Crusader jet from Los Angeles to New York City in 3 hours and 23 minutes. Glenn's flight shaved more than 20 minutes off the previous record.

For a man who had always loved airplanes and speed, the United States space program came along at just the right time. Less than three months after Glenn broke the cross-country speed record, the Soviet Union launched the first man-made satellite, *Sputnik 1*, into orbit around Earth. The United States quickly shifted its space program into high gear to try to catch up with the Soviets. Nearly four months after the flight of *Sputnik 1*, America sent *Explorer 1* soaring into orbit. For the next few years, both countries launched more and more complex rockets and satellites. The goal was to be the first country to put a human being into orbit.

The National Aeronautics and Space Administration (NASA) was created by the United States in 1958. At the top of their agenda was a search for America's first astronauts. They were looking for men who had at least 1,500 hours of flying time, had test pilot experience, and were less than 40 years old. More than 100 men, including John Glenn, met all of the criteria. No women were eligible to become astronauts at the time.

All of the candidates were given rigorous physical and psychological tests. Finally, the names of America's first seven astronauts were announced on April 9, 1959. They were:

Navy Lieutenant Malcolm Scott Carpenter
Air Force Captain Leroy Gordon Cooper

Marine Lieutenant Colonel John Herschel Glenn
Air Force Captain Virgil "Gus" Grissom
Navy Lieutenant Commander Walter M. Schirra
Navy Lieutenant Commander Alan B. Shepard
Air Force Captain Donald K. Slayton

These seven men were known as the Mercury 7, after the Mercury capsules they would fly into space. The American public hailed the astronauts as heroes who were willing to sacrifice their lives in the interest of space exploration. The men would be riding on top of blazing rockets, the same kind of

The Mercury 7 (from left to right): Schirra, Shepard, Grissom, Slayton, Glenn, Carpenter, and Cooper.

rockets that had blown up on the launchpad many times in the past.

Once the excitement settled down, the men had to get busy and learn how to be astronauts. While they were training, NASA administrators tackled the difficult job of deciding who would go into space first. Alan Shepard was chosen to ride in the first Mercury capsule. Less than one month before Shepard's scheduled liftoff, the Soviets blasted Yuri Gagarin into orbit aboard *Vostok 1*, on April 12, 1961. After Gagarin's successful flight, John Glenn said, "They just beat the pants off us. . . . But now that the space age has begun, there's going to be plenty of work for everybody."

Alan Shepard and Gus Grissom made successful suborbital flights in 1961, putting America back in the space race. The first two U.S. astronauts did not go into orbit, but each flew more than 100 miles (161 kilometers) high in order to test equipment and procedures. John Glenn was selected to fly the third mission, the one that would put an American astronaut in orbit.

Glenn's Mercury capsule, *Friendship 7*, was scheduled for liftoff on February 20, 1962. On that day, the 40-year-old astronaut got up at 2:30 in the morning, ate breakfast, and put on his space suit. After a bus ride to Launchpad 14, Glenn was strapped into his seat in the tiny spacecraft. For more than three hours he lay on his back and looked at the sky through the capsule's one small window. When the final countdown began, fellow Mercury astronaut Scott Carpenter said to his friend, "Godspeed, John Glenn."

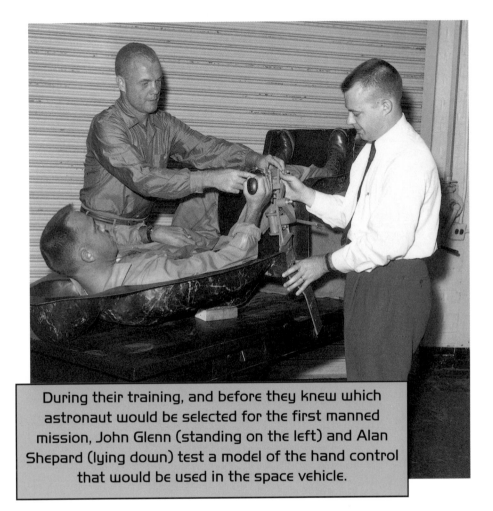

During their training, and before they knew which astronaut would be selected for the first manned mission, John Glenn (standing on the left) and Alan Shepard (lying down) test a model of the hand control that would be used in the space vehicle.

As the countdown reached zero, the Atlas rocket slowly rumbled to life. Glenn said, "I could feel the engines start. The spacecraft shook, not violently but very solidly. There was no doubt when liftoff occurred. When the Atlas was released there was an immediate gentle surge that let you know you were on your way."

★ ASTRONAUT TESTING ★

NASA's first astronaut candidates were given rigorous physical and psychological tests to measure their endurance. In the late 1950s, space exploration was just beginning and nobody knew what would happen to human beings in weightlessness. NASA wanted to be sure its astronauts were tough and ready to face the unknown, so they put them through a battery of tests including the following:

★ The men were locked in dark, soundproof rooms for varying lengths of time.

★ A giant centrifuge, which is a machine that spins faster and faster, was used to see if the men could withstand the pressures of liftoff and reentry.

★ Their ears were bombarded with very high-frequency sounds until their bodies shook.

★ They were strapped into a vibrating machine and then expected to press certain buttons and flip switches faster and faster.

★ Astronaut candidates were taken up in a C-131 transport plane. As the plane flew up and down like a roller coaster, the passengers experienced several seconds of weightlessness. The motion made many astronauts sick, so the plane was nicknamed the "Vomit Comet."

After each test, blood pressure readings and heart rates were measured to see how each candidate handled stress.

Friendship 7 and the Atlas rocket that will carry it into orbit blast off from Cape Canaveral, Florida, on February 20, 1962, with John Glenn aboard.

The beaches and roads around Cape Canaveral were filled with people watching as the Atlas rocketed skyward. All over America, radios and television sets were tuned into live broadcasts of the launch. In New York City's Grand Central Station, the loudspeakers announced that Colonel Glenn had just blasted off. The voice added: "Please say a prayer for him." No American had ever gone into orbit before. Could he survive this trip into the unknown? John Glenn's wife and children watched the liftoff on television from their home in Arlington, Virginia.

As the spacecraft raced higher and higher, John Glenn was pressed back into his seat by a force nearly eight times the gravity on Earth, making his body feel like it weighed nearly a ton. Finally, after a rough 7-minute ride, the pressure let up and the spacecraft entered orbit going 17,500 miles (28,175 kilometers) per hour. John Glenn said to those in Mission Control, "Zero-g, and I feel fine." When the capsule turned around and Glenn got his first look at Earth, he exclaimed, "Oh, that view is tremendous!"

Glenn felt fine, but how was his body holding up in weightlessness? Scientists were not sure that astronauts would be able to even see or swallow in space. In order to test his eyes, Glenn read from a chart several times during the mission. He also moved his head around to see if it made him dizzy. Then he tried eating a tube of applesauce to see if he could swallow and digest food. He reported, "This is *Friendship 7*. Have eaten one tube of food. . . . I've had no problem eating." He also told those on Earth, "I have had no ill effects at all as yet from any zero-g. It's very pleasant, in fact visual acuity is still excellent. . . . Head movements caused no nausea or discomfort whatsoever. Over."

While John Glenn was performing his experiments and enjoying the scenery below, the engineers at Mission Control were in a panic. Just after liftoff, a light on one of the ground computers flashed, indicating the spacecraft's landing bag had deployed early. This was a major problem because the capsule's heat shield was attached to the landing bag. If the heat shield had come free, John Glenn would not have any protection from the blazing temperatures during reentry. Without a heat shield, *Friendship 7* would burn up as it came back to Earth. The engineers hoped that the problem was only a faulty signal light, but nobody knew for sure. As they frantically looked for answers, the flight of *Friendship 7* continued.

Glenn, flying 162 miles (261 kilometers) above Earth, was unaware of the heat-shield problem. At two and a half hours

★ MYSTERIOUS PARTICLES ★

Just after John Glenn's first orbit in *Friendship 7*, he looked out of the window and saw sparkling particles floating around the capsule. He reported to Mission Control, "I'll try to describe what I'm in here. I am in a big mass of some very small particles that are brilliantly lit up like they're luminescent. I never saw anything like it. . . . They swirl around the capsule and go in front of the window and they're all brilliantly lighted." As Glenn watched he said, "They drift by the window and I can see them against the dark sky. Just at sunrise there were literally thousands of them." Each time *Friendship 7* passed from night into day, the glittering particles swirled around the capsule.

Scientists later figured out that the particles were caused by moisture from the spacecraft. As air was vented outside, the moisture froze into tiny ice crystals that were visible only at dawn.

into the flight, Mission Control asked him: "Do you still consider yourself GO for the next orbit?" Glenn replied, "That is affirmative. I am GO for the next orbit." As the capsule was due to pass over Perth, Australia, many of the residents of that city turned on their porch and car lights. Since it was night at the time, thousands of lights were visible to Glenn. He said to Mission Control, "The lights show up very well. Thank everybody for turning them on, will you?"

Friendship 7 was scheduled for seven orbits, but those on the ground were worried about the heat shield and decided to bring the capsule down early. They advised Glenn that the trip would be cut short and then began the reentry countdown. As John Glenn fired the retro-rockets that would help him come back to Earth, he said, "I could hear each rocket fire and could feel the surge as the rockets slowed the spacecraft."

Normally the used rockets were released before reentry. Instead of releasing the rockets, though, Glenn was asked to leave them attached to the capsule. Ground controllers hoped the rockets would help keep the heat shield in place. About 2 minutes before reentry, John Glenn was told that his landing bag may have broken free during liftoff. It didn't take him long to figure out that his heat shield may have also been damaged.

Glenn said that during reentry, "...there was a noise and a bump on the spacecraft. I saw one of the straps that hold the retro-rocket package swing in front of the window. . . . Flaming pieces were breaking off and flying past the spacecraft window. . . . I thought these flaming pieces might be parts of the heat shield breaking off." Glenn radioed: "This is *Friendship 7*. A real fireball outside."

For the next three minutes during reentry, there was the normal communications blackout. Those on the ground were sweating while they waited to hear if John Glenn survived his trip back to Earth. As Mission Control continued to radio: "How do you read? How do you read?" to *Friendship 7*, they finally heard Glenn say, "Loud and clear." Cheers erupted at Cape Canaveral when Glenn's voice came over the intercom. The heat shield had performed its job and kept the capsule and its passenger safe during reentry.

Friendship 7 splashed down in the Pacific Ocean, ending the 5-hour pioneering flight of John Glenn. A helicopter picked up the spacecraft and carried it to the deck of the destroyer *Noa*. A very hot John Glenn took no time getting out of the 100-degree heat inside the capsule. After a shower, some food, and a few medical tests, Glenn was on his way to the Bahamas for a reunion with some of his fellow Mercury astronauts.

Then it was on to Florida, where Glenn was reunited with Annie. The couple rode in a convertible from the airport to Cape Canaveral while thousands of people along the road cheered and waved American flags. America's first orbiting astronaut was an instant hero! During the following weeks, parades were held all over the country to honor John Glenn. One of the biggest parades was held in New York City, along the 16-block-long "Canyon of Heroes."

President John F. Kennedy considered John Glenn to be a national treasure. Kennedy quietly let it be known to NASA

Soon after his historic flight, John Glenn was honored with a ticker-tape parade through New York City's Canyon of Heroes. Sitting in the back of the car with him are Annie and Vice President Lyndon B. Johnson.

administrators that Glenn's life should not be risked in another mission. Glenn knew nothing about this request and planned to continue his astronaut career by training for a mission to the moon. When his name was not put on any future crew lists, Glenn got very frustrated and resigned from the astronaut corps in 1964. From then on, John Glenn could only watch as others explored space. His wife, Annie, said, "He's wanted to go on every flight since then [*Friendship 7*]."

John earned a Distinguished Service Cross for his pioneering space flight. At the awards ceremony on March 1, 1962, he sits with President John F. Kennedy.

After leaving the space program, John Glenn remained in the Marines and did some consulting work for NASA. He retired from the Marine Corps in 1965 and became an executive at Royal Crown Cola. In 1968 he decided to try his hand at politics and ran for a seat in the United States Senate. He was defeated in that election but won the seat in 1974. For the next 24 years, John Glenn served as a senator from the state of Ohio.

He was a candidate during the 1984 presidential primaries but did not win a spot on the Democratic ticket.

During his years in Washington, Glenn was a member of the Senate Special Committee on Aging. While he was

★ SENATOR JOHN GLENN ★

In 1974, soon-to-be-Senator Glenn lets his tie tell people what he'd like them to do.

During John Glenn's 24 years in the United States Senate, he participated in more than 9,500 roll-call votes. In addition to voting on important government matters, he worked very hard to reduce the number of nuclear weapons in the world. He also stressed the need to clean up contamination at American nuclear production plants.

In addition to his work to limit nuclear weapons, John Glenn often voted for bills that supported scientific and technical programs. He served on a committee that studied the problems elderly people face concerning social security benefits and medical problems. Glenn also worked to encourage reforms in government spending and campaign finance during his four terms in the United States Senate.

reviewing some of the documents for his committee work, he read that older people suffer from some of the same problems as astronauts in weightlessness. Both experience such things as sleep problems, bone and muscle weakness, and dizziness. After thinking about the similarities, he said, "I figured we could learn a lot if we sent an older person up [in space], studied what the effects of weightlessness were, and tried to learn what turns these body systems on and off."

In the summer of 1996, John Glenn got in touch with NASA administrator Dan Goldin and told him, "…there are 34 million Americans over 65, and that's due to triple in the next 50 years. And I told him someone ought to look into this." The someone Glenn had in mind was himself. He had never stopped wanting another flight into space. He was 75 years old, and time was running out.

On January 15, 1997, Dan Goldin called Glenn's Senate office with great news. He said the mission was GO if Glenn could pass the flight physical and complete the same training as the rest of the crew. An elated John Glenn lost no time in accepting Goldin's offer of a shuttle mission. Before he began training in Houston, though, Glenn announced that he would retire from the Senate when his term ended in 1998.

With his Senate career winding down, John Glenn was anxious to become an astronaut once again. He reported for duty at Johnson Space Center in Houston, Texas, and passed the medical tests with flying colors. Glenn had stayed in shape by eating light, power walking 2 miles (3 kilometers) a day, and lifting weights. During the next few months, Glenn trained for the mission with his much younger crewmates. Curt Brown,

John Glenn gives a thumbs-up to his fellow senators as President Bill Clinton introduced him during the 1998 State of the Union address. The president announced that Glenn would be part of the next space shuttle mission, and that Glenn would be the oldest person to travel in space.

commander of the *Discovery* mission, had been just five years old when Glenn first orbited Earth in 1962.

John Glenn had a great deal to learn about the shuttle's operating systems and emergency procedures. He was also assigned to take many of the pictures during the flight and had to know how to operate all of the cameras on board *Discovery*. Curt Brown jokingly said, "He [Glenn] was happy to come fly with us. . . . But he may not be happy after a few days in orbit. We plan to work him to the bone."

When all of the training had been completed, the crew was ready to put their skills to the test. After a successful liftoff on October 29, 1998, Curt Brown was able to report that John Glenn was once again in orbit, 36 years after his historic first flight.

UPON REACHING ORBIT, JOHN GLENN AND THE CREW TOOK A few minutes to get used to being weightless. Then they had to go to work. They folded up the extra seats, changed clothes, and began unpacking some of the 83 experiments on board. The crew had a wide range of things to do—from studying the balance mechanisms in the ears of toadfish to deploying a Spartan satellite that would study the sun.

Many of the experiments concerned John Glenn and his body's reaction to weightlessness. On board *Discovery*, Glenn would be poked and prodded, and his blood taken ten times by Scott Parazynski. Glenn joked, "Scott's taken my blood so many times that when I see him I say, 'Here comes Dracula.' " In addition to the bloodletting, John Glenn wore 21 sensors

Glenn uses an electronic still camera to take a picture of
Earth through a window in the space shuttle.
Photographing his home planet was just one of the jobs
for which Glenn had to train before his return to space.

attached to his head while he slept to measure his sleep patterns and brain waves. Data collected in orbit would be compared with data gathered before and after the mission. Scientists hoped to learn more about the aging process by studying the results of Glenn's tests.

In addition to being a human experiment, Glenn also had many jobs to perform during the nine-day mission. He was a full-fledged member of the crew and was expected to work right along with the others. When they were not working, the *Discovery* astronauts enjoyed looking out of the windows at Earth below. On one pass over Australia, the people of Perth turned on all of their lights, just as they had done in 1962. John Glenn said, "It looks even brighter now than it did back then. . . . It looks beautiful."

Before long, the nine-day mission of *Discovery* was over. John Glenn and the crew packed up their experiments, put on their launch/entry suits, and strapped into their seats. Steve Lindsey fired rockets to slow the shuttle and then pointed its nose at Earth. Gravity did the rest.

The shuttle has no power of its own during landing. It is like a big glider falling from the sky. Once the landing is started there is no way to correct the course. But *Discovery's* landing at Kennedy Space Center on November 7, 1998, was perfect. When the shuttle had rolled to a stop, the crew took a little time to get their Earth legs back. John Glenn was nauseated and threw up a few times before walking out of the shuttle. It was the only time in the mission he felt sick. He later said, "I didn't feel too hot went I got off." Glenn recovered quickly, though, and was all smiles when greeted by his family.

On November 7, 1998, *Discovery* touched down
at Kennedy Space Center in Florida, ending John Glenn's
second historic flight in space.

Just as in 1962, John was honored with a parade in New York City's Canyon of Heroes with Annie at his side.

After the return of *Discovery*, John Glenn was met with the same kind of enthusiasm as after his first flight. He and the rest of the crew rode in a parade along the Canyon of Heroes that rivaled the one in 1962. Driving the convertible that carried John and Annie Glenn was a New York City police officer whose dad had driven the couple in 1962. Annie Glenn said, "John has just been taken aback by the intense outpouring of love and pride. These are memories you keep forever. . . ."

In an interview after the successful touchdown of *Discovery*, John Glenn was asked what it was like to float in space. He replied, "It was fun! I was able to float around and spin. But there is nothing to stop you once you start moving. I banged my head a couple of times." A student wanted to know what path to take to become an astronaut. Glenn told him, "The best advice for people who want to be astronauts is to study hard and do the best they can in school. Astronauts-to-be should focus especially on science and math, but other subjects are important, too."

When asked if he would ever return to space, John Glenn replied, "I would imagine this will probably be my last flight." He did have this to say about his mission, though:

I've noticed that maybe because of all this, people are seeing themselves in a way they haven't before. They're realizing that older people have the same ambitions, hopes, and dreams as anybody else. I say you should live life based on how you feel and not by the calendar.

★ IMPORTANT DATES ★

1921	John Glenn born in Cambridge, Ohio, on July 18.
1939	Graduates from New Concord High School; enrolls in Muskingum College.
1941	Earns a pilot's license; joins the United States Navy.
1943	Glenn earns his Navy wings; marries Annie Castor on April 6.
1944	Flies 59 missions in the Pacific during World War II.
1945	Son David born on December 13.
1947	Daughter Carolyn (Lyn) born on March 19.
1950–1953	Flies 90 missions during Korean War.
1954	Graduates from test pilot school.
1957	Breaks airplane cross-country speed record; Russian satellite *Sputnik 1* orbits Earth on October 4.

1959	Becomes one of America's first seven astronauts.
1962	Becomes first American to orbit Earth on February 20.
1965	Retires from the Marine Corps.
1974	Elected to the United States Senate.
1980	Elected to a second Senate term.
1986	Elected to a third Senate term.
1992	Elected to a fourth Senate term.
1997	Announces his retirement from the Senate when his term ends in 1998.
1998	Becomes the oldest person to fly in space.

★ FURTHER READING ★

Bredeson, Carmen. *Our Space Program.* Brookfield, CT: The Millbrook Press, 1999.

Bredeson, Carmen. *Shannon Lucid: Space Ambassador.* Brookfield, CT: The Millbrook Press, 1999.

Campbell, Ann-Jeanette. *Amazing Space: A Book of Answers for Kids.* New York: John Wiley & Sons, Inc., 1997.

Cole, Michael. *Friendship 7: First American in Orbit.* Springfield, NJ: Enslow Publishers, Inc., 1995.

Montgomery, Scott, and Timothy Gaffney. *Back in Orbit: John Glenn's Return to Space.* Atlanta: Longstreet Press, Inc., 1998.

Mulland, R. Mike. *Do Your Ears Pop in Space?* New York: John Wiley & Sons, Inc., 1997.

Ride, Sally. *To Space and Back.* New York: Lothrop, Lee & Shepard Books, 1986.

★ NASA INTERNET SITES ★

www.nasa.gov
NASA's home page

www.ksc.nasa.gov/history/history.html
Hitorical archive of spaceflight and manned missions

eol.jsc.nasa.gov
The Earth Sciences home page of Johnson Space Center contains
astronauts' photos of Earth.

www.jpl.nasa.gov
The home page of NASA's Jet Propulsion Laboratory contains
information on robotic explorations of the solar system.

images.jsc.nasa.gov
NASA images

★ INDEX ★